The Santa Spirit

Dedicated to kichle

The Santa Spirit

ISBN: 978-1-7358304-2-1 (hardcover)
978-1-7358304-3-8 (ebook)

Published by
Vissing and Associates LLC

Design by: Darlene Swanson • www.van-garde.com

Why is
Santa Claus
special?

Santa Claus *might* bring presents, but . . .

the most important thing he brings is the Santa Spirit.

If someone gives us a
present they share the
Santa Spirit.

When we make
or give friends a
present we share the
Santa Spirit.

You can find the Santa Spirit in nice feelings we get inside, like love, excitement and joy.

Surprise

Friends

Gentleness

Family

Kindness

Ziemassvētku vecītis (Latvia)

Jultomten (Sweden)

Jólasveina (Iceland)

Дед Мороз Ded Moroz (Russia)

Shengdan laoren 聖誕老人 (China)

Inuit - Quviasukvik spirit

Święty Mikołaj (Poland)

Ayoz Bobo (Uzbekistan)

Canada - Pere Noel

Bodach na Nollaig (Scotland)

Daidí na Nollag (Ireland)

Siôn Corn (Wales)

Le Père Noël (France)

Weihnachtsmann (Germany)

Babbo Natale (Italy)

US - Santa Claus

Şaxta Baba (Azerbaijan)

Noel Baba (Turkey)

산타 클로스 (Korea)

Mexico - Niño Dios

Africa - Mama Tinga Tinga

Ông Già Nô-en (Vietnam

San Nicolás (Costa Rica)

Nigeria - Santa Claus

Brazil - Bom Velhinho

Viejito Pascuero (Chile)

South Africa -- Kersvader

Everywhere on the planet you can find the spirit of Santa!
Santa goes by different names and faces in different places.

Where does Santa live? He might live at the North Pole.

Did you know there is a North Pole in Alaska, Idaho, Oklahoma, New York, and even Australia? Others think Santa is from Iceland, Scandinavia, or Canada.

So long the Santa spirit lives in your heart,

Santa can live anywhere!

All around
the world people
celebrate winter
festivals

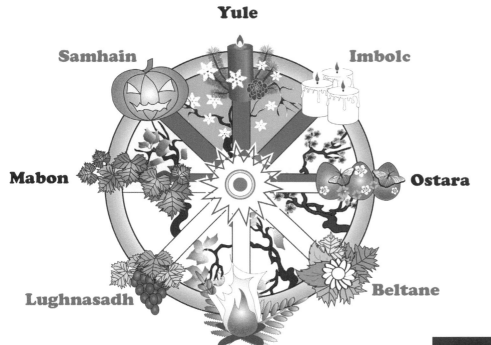

Yule

Samhain

Imbolc

Mabon

Ostara

Lughnasadh

Beltane

Midsummer

Many December festivals are around the winter solstice, the shortest-day longest-night of the year.

These festivals embody Santa's spirit of fun, joy, togetherness and hope.

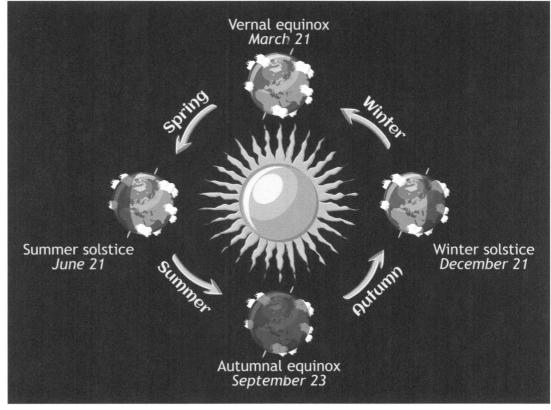

Vernal equinox
March 21

Spring

Winter

Summer solstice
June 21

Winter solstice
December 21

Summer

Autumn

Autumnal equinox
September 23

In ancient times Nordic god Odin flew through the sky on his 8-legged white horse, Sleipnir, bringing gifts to children.

Another Nordic god, Thor, traveled in a chariot across the sky pulled by two white goats. He put fruit and candy in shoes children left by the fireplace.

Both had long white beards and liked the color red.

King Frost, Lord Snow and Father Winter
were wise and helped people make merry
during cold, dark seasons
in Europe and Great Britain.

Long ago in Turkey, Hagios Nikolaos left gifts of gold and treats in the stockings of children at night while they slept. Church people respected him so much they made him a saint.

Sometimes Santa is called St. Nicholas.

Santas can be women too.

La Befana flies over Italy rooftops and slips down chimneys to bring children presents from a big basket she carries.

St. Lucy gives children gifts in Sweden.

Snegurochka delivers children gifts with her grandfather, Ded Moroz, the Russian Santa.

Mama Tinga Tinga is the African Santa Claus. Any woman with a beautiful heart and kind acts can be a Santa.

What does Santa wear?

Most people think that Santa
wears a fuzzy red suit because
he lives in a cold climate.

But in hot countries he
might wear shorts!

He might wear brown, green, or any color.

The Santa Spirit isn't found in what people wear –

it is found in the kindness of their heart.

Santa could be old or young, tall or short,
chubby, or skinny, girl or boy.

Santa could have any color of skin and speak any language.

It doesn't matter
what you look
like so long
as you have the
Santa Spirit inside.

How Does Santa Travel?

In a sleigh pulled by tiny reindeer? Or in a horse-drawn cart?

In Australia, his sleigh is pulled by kangaroos!

In Brazil he comes in a helicopter.

Other places by airplane. And in Belgium he arrives by boat!

In many places,
he walks to
deliver presents.

Santa finds a way
to come to people
who believe in him.

What Does Santa Bring?

Santa might bring a few little presents
to put in stockings or shoes.

His sleigh and pack are small.

He can't carry many or big things.

He is happy when people remember
that others deserve presents too.

Santa knows sharing is caring.

Santa likes when you leave
him and his reindeer treats or
thank-you notes.

The Attitude of Gratitude is
part of the Spirit of Santa.

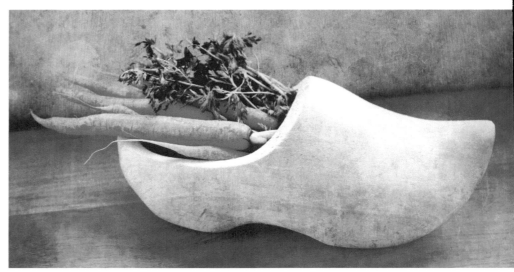

Imagination is part of the Santa Spirit.

Do you ever wonder how Santa's reindeer fly,
how he can squeeze down chimneys, and
how he knows what you like?

Writing a letter to Santa helps us to figure out what we really want.

When we know what we want we can figure out
how to make our dreams come true.

Making dreams come true is part of the spirit of Santa.

Santa needs
helpers to deliver
gifts and spread the
Santa Spirit.

Your family, friends,
and neighbors
might be
Santa's elves.

Santa knows we
need others to
accomplish
good things.

You can be a Santa elf too!

You feel the Santa Spirit when you help others
make presents or tell people that you care.

Family and friends are Santa's best helpers.

When they spend time with you they may show the Santa Spirit.

It would be hard for Santa to do his job without them.

When we make others happy, we feel happy too.

It is the Santa Spirit at work!

Love is the Spirit of Santa.

When love surrounds you know that the Santa Spirit is there.

You can find Santa's spirit in your heart
no matter who you are.

Santa will live forever

As long as you believe!

Could the impossible
be possible?

Dream

Plan

Believe in the power of the Santa Spirit

PICTURE CREDITS*

(in order of appearance)

Cover: Santa in sleigh   vectorfusionart

Red Santa arms outstretched Milles Studio

Family watching sleigh over moon Yuganov Konstantin

Wide-eyed baby EvgeniiAnd

Mother and child fizkes

Child in hat Sunny studio

Surprised girl Yuliia D

Family reading Jack Frog

Baby sleeping Yarkovoy

Santa opening box TierneyMJ

Santa with map of the world Ollyy

Chinese family at table animicsgo

Parade of multi-religious people Aleutie

Kwanza CDGROUPS

Lohri stockillustration

Diwali littleWhale

Hanukah Maglara

Wheel of the Year   Snowbelle

Seasons Inna Bigun

Blue Odin   patrimonio designs ltd

Black & White god Morphart Creation

Thor Liliya Butenko

Snowy Santa g215

Santa with children   Victorian Traditions

Santa Victorian Traditions

St. Nicholas drawing   Alexander Donchev

Human dressed as St. Nicholas Breedfoto

Befana NGvozdeva

St. Lucy bluejeans

Snegurochka bellerebelle_n

North Pole map   Franzi

Graphic Santa   Aleksangel

Santa with surfboard   Christos Georghiou

Traditional, tree over shoulder Victorian Traditions

Traditional with tree Victorian Traditions

Santa in blue Teni

Santa in knickers NGvozdeva

Child on belly   Photographerivanova

Graphic Santa with bell Helen Stebakov

Skinny Santa Ozric Dillon

Graphic Santa & child in chair imagetico

Graphic Mrs. Claus   jazzerup

Santa & children reading   Lucky Business

Peek-a-boo with dad George Rudy

Children holding box   zenstock

Shirtless child in Santa hat   Luis Louro

Santa head Milles Studio

Santa at beach   TinyDoz

Running Santas   Zubada

Santa around the world Yauhen Paleski

Santa & sleigh, blue sky LoopAll

Santa horse cart Zhanna Smolyar

Santa and helicopter Boguslaw Mazur

Santa and kangas Binly

Santa and boat Dennis Cox

Santa and plane DRogatnev

Santa walking in snow Victorian Traditions

Santa reindeer blue mollicart

Wooden shoes Suzanne Tucker

Santa stocking Victorian Traditions

Milk and cookies mikeledray

Carrots in shoe Suzanne Tucker

Family watching sky Yuganov Konstantin

Writing to Santa   wavebreakmedia

Faces HelgaLin

Santa and elf Evgeny Atamanenko

Family at table DGLimages

Family with presents Monkey Business Images

Mom making cookies Evgeny Atamanenko

Dad and child decorating tree   bbernard

Dog love 4 PM production

Girl friends weedezign

Men with child tommaso lizzul

Grandparents & book Lucky Business

Hand heart everst

Girl with happy heart fizkes

Mom, girl and heart fizkes

Santa and child on roof Yuganov Konstantin

Jumping on the bed 4 PM production

Grandpa with children Monkey Business Images

Siblings and present Yuganov Konstantin

Gold moon ingibiork

Sparkle sleigh Senoldo

Girl reading book Mimma Key

Gold swirl Tori Art

Cut-out of Santa face Magi Bagi

Child with box and lights Sergey Nivens

5 children looking in box   2xSamara.com

Mother and child with box, lights Inara Prusakova

Mother and daughter with box Prostock-studio

2 Children with box alexkich

Christmas town DRogatnev

Igloo festival nataka

Golden woman Subbotina Anna

Heart world Milena Moiola

Magic in your hands Romolo Tavani

These pictures were purchased from Shutterstock with approval to use them in this book. The author wishes to express gratitude to the photographers and graphic artists who contributed to the beauty of this book. Thanks for sharing the Santa Spirt with our readers!

You have the
power of the
Santa Spirit in
your hands